D1706942

GIULIANO KREMMERZ

ANGELS AND DEMONS OF LOVE

EDITED AND TRANSLATED BY CRISTIAN GUZZO

BRINDISI 2019

Giuliano Kremmerz

FOREWORD

Angels and Demons of Love was published in 1898 by the Neapolitan publisher Detken & Rocholl[1]. This work was part of a wider project to disseminate the occult sciences in Italy, which Giuliano Kremmerz (alias Ciro Formisano, 1861-1930) undertook with the publication of the famous magazine *Mondo Secreto* (The Secret World), edited in Naples between 1896 and 1899.

This publication, in addition to making extensive propaganda of magic and to address critically the problem of spirit phenomena, became the official propaganda organ of the *Fratellanza Terapeutico-Magica di Miriam*.

Kremmerz, alchemist and therapeutist, founded, in 1899, after an alleged sojourn in southern America, the *Schola Philosophica Hermetica Classica Italica Fratellanza Terapeutica Magica di Miriam*.

Following the teachings of his mentor Izar Bne Escur (Pasquale de Servis, 1818-1893), who traced his lineage back to the pre-Christian hermetic traditions of the Italian peninsula, Ciro Formisano founded Miriamic academies in many Italian cities, including Rome, Naples, Bari and La Spezia, with the sole aim of applying the ancient hermetic sciences to 'medicine, therapeutics, psychurgy and thaumaturgy, with the intention of healing the sick through occult medicine.

The Brotherhood was an external emanation of the *Egyptian Grand Orient*. It was a masonic and magical structure that pursued the so-called high *osiridea* initiation that involved

---

[1] The book has been printed ten times: 1917 (Società Editrice Partenopea), 1921 (Società Editrice Partenopea), 1946 and 1947 (Società Editrice Partenopea), 1954 (Ceur Edizioni), 1975 (Edizioni Mediterranee), 1987 (two editions; Fratelli Melita, I Dioscuri), 1992 (Circolo Virgiliano) and 2000 (Edizioni Rebis).

the use of sexual alchemy and ceremonial magic with the invocation of disincarnate intelligences belonging to the Chaldean or better Mesopotamian Egyptian pantheon. In order to practice the internal alchemy or sexual magic, a long process of purification from selfishness and profane materialism was necessary, which was accomplished through the practice of occult therapy.

The doing of good, healing a sick person through individual and collective practices, benefited the sick and, at the same time the practitioner toot, rooting him on the path of high magic. A good part of Kremmerz's literary production was aimed at illustrating his theories about magic therapeutics, while *Angels and Demons of Love* is the first attempt to write about profane and sacred love, highlighting the importance of Catholic mass as the ritual containing the true essence of sexual magic.

The work is largely influenced by the French occult milieu and the language is often archaic and enigmatic. However, this book is the first evidence of the presence of sexual practices connected with spirituality, already at the end of the nineteenth century and therefore a long time before Georges Le Clément De Saint-Marcq wrote his own work entitled *L'Eucharistie* (1906). Kremmerz died in Beuasoleil in 1930 and today his ideas and theories are carried out by some kremmerzian associations, who practice the occult medicine and, in internal circles, sexual alchemy.

Brindisi, March 06, 2019

Cristian Guzzo

Under an old portrait of Giuseppe Balsamo everyone could read: *Pour savoir ce qu'il est, the faudrait être lui même*. To know what love is, you must love. Vain is every definition of this indefinable feeling, on which the whole history of the living and the dead is embroidered: vain every philosophy and every art that deals with it as to close this topic in a precise and concrete disposition or suffering of the human soul.

The love for a doctor is the sensual desire of the male for the female and vice versa: for the anthropologist is the memory that perpetuates itself in the animal instinct of the act of procreation from which we are all originated: for the poet is a canticle of the poem of God: for the ascetic is the desire for good: so on and on.

For occult science, LOVE IS THE INSTINCTIVE SACRIFICE, UNDER THE MOST VARIED FORMS, OF THE EGO IN THE SYNTHETIC UNITY OF NATURE; and, as this synthesis of Nature, all peoples impersonate it in God, the feeling of love, however explicit or felt, is divine[2].

From here, those who want to trace the religious conceptions of all time, manifested in the cults of all the nations of the world, must go on examining how much the altars or tabernacles and ancient mysteries hid to the profane. As there is no act of earthly life, from the chemical law that determines love in unorganized bodies to the physical reproduction of the beast that is animal love, which does not

---

[2] Love without sacrifice of himself or part of himself, is nonsense. Those who say they love without giving their self to lover, do not love. Those who sacrifice themselves to the beloved person perform the greatest act of love. Jealousy, a restrictive feeling of love for possession; it is not a witness of love, because it desires the opposite of love: it is the victim of the desire for freedom of affection of the person whom one loves.

have and does not receive the impression of the sacrifice of unity for unity of the universe, so there is no classical religion that has not foundation in the loving instincts of the things generated by their generator, of nature-matter for the nature God.

Modern civilization has broken down the ancient savage customs of the aborigines: man physically and spiritually is evolving and not fully evolved, nor is it essentially modified. The savage state and advanced civilization act on man with the burden of needs and needs, in relation to the times, modified by the conditions of the people and of their constituted unities.

The transformer of every being is the love for his own kind, that the foolish profane philosophy, whose masters did not see beyond matter, it did not admit that under the appearance of an *innate idea* of the conservation of the species, false and materialistic belief in an idea that is not innate at all, to perpetuate this magnificent race of not winged bipeds[3]. Civilization tool is love.

Where love does not exist, the exception to civilization is manifest. Vico, in his New Science, deals with it profoundly, mentioning the conceit of nations. And the whole history of human glories must be sought in the

---

[3] In practice, with modern demographic studies, we see how false this commonplace of vulgar philosophy is. The advanced men limit the offspring, the not advanced suffer the consequence of the animal act; and the most brutal born criminals get rid of it with violence. Among the most civilized who cleverly try to limit offspring and violent people who defy human justice, the act of delinquency is the same if one wants to believe that it is a social crime, that is *against society*, to take away the life of its unities. The love for the offspring, when the offspring is not in the mind to any of the spouses or individuals who make their functions, is perfectly absent. In stealthy loves, if an idea reigns, it is the fear of offspring. But the concept of the perpetuation of the species is religious, religiously transmitted in the peoples in which philosophy has not thrown the sacerdotal truths in meal to the animal passions of the crowds.

subsequent development of this spiritual feeling in the lives of families, nations and peoples.

The title of this writing is beautiful, and I must write dryly, because the science of love must not be confused with the art that sings love. I write its anatomy, for men and women who want to study deeply and progress in the knowledge of the scientific truth of human life, to scan, in a more distant time, in the law that regulates the feeling of divine love.

This anatomy of love, which certainly will not be reproduced in the theatre of a hospital, I begin by making my readers understand that other people, and the most famous than me have done, before me. Dante Alighieri who was not even half understood by the multitude of his grammarian commentators, has made the analysis of love on several occasions, while singing it as one of the later poets who wrote about it, to amuse some Beatrice of flesh and tendons, quivering for sensual kisses[4].

Dante, like the neoplatonists his precursors and contemporaries, was an initiate into the high verities of divine magic, an occultist, as we would say today, but of those who could be greeted as poets in the ancient way, when the orphic initiation had transmitted in the Western world the secret of singing for the people, in the form of flat and allegorical forms, the most secret truths of the initiatory sanctuary.

The common person, that is the intellectually infant man, stops himself in front of the literal meaning of the written or sung words; just as the child who, happy with the appearance of things, does not scan the content or the reason of them.

---

[4] Program of the *Mondo Secreto*, 1897.

The advanced man, master of human philosophy, that is a relative and not absolute matter, tries to penetrate the *allegorical* sense, that is always in relation to human knowledge and known facts. But the initiate to the secrets of the divine word, that is, to the verities coming from a world where it is not possible to get in, if not naturally and intellectually evolving, he anagogically reads, in ancient classical poets and philosophers, the most celestial and natural arcana[5].

Francesco Perez who is the only modern commentator who has grasped the hidden sense of Beatrice in Dante, writes *beatrice* with the smallest *b* because he says that «*the beatrice must allegorically mean something that the man sane of mind can say that, respect to love for her, that love for philosophy is cowardly and evil desire*». But not only this: *she must be such a thing* FOR WHICH ONLY THE HUMAN SPECIES SURPASSES ALL THAT THE TERRESTRIAL GLOBE CONTAINS.

O donna di virtù, sola per cui
L'umana specie eccede ogni contento
Da quel ciel che ha minor li cerchi sui.

---

[5] The language of ancient poets was the sacred- and the science of interpretation of classical books really for their form and content, belongs to the highest of the initiatory temple. The Bible, even in its most recent books, should be interpreted like this and then unveiled to the astonished people, to see the so many blunders taken by Loke's translators despising the natural philosophy of Genesis. Virgil and Homer wrote in the same way about ancient sacred things: the whole Trojan epopee and the arrival on the Lazio beaches of the people of Aeneas, is a sacred history of occult philosophy, of which, writing today, there would certainly not be a audience of ten people able to understand it. In this regard, I read a jeratic translation of the *Cantica dei Cantici* made by Mr. Justinian Lebano, learnedly accomplished with an examination of sacred language; but how many have understood it?

Now, however the illustrious Sicilian may refer to the allegory of the beatrice, hiding the Wisdom of the Elects, while the commons people of philosophers does not go beyond the profane interpretation of Aristotelian and Platonic *Intelligence*, nor the commons people can penetrate into the sublime interpretation of the essence of this intelligence, which is not the deceptive human reason, on which sensist experimentalism erects its castle of papier-mache, in its reflections, reflecting the problems of the spirit of man. In his *Vita Nova*, Dante says:

Amor e cor gentile sono una cosa
Sì come il saggio in suo dittato pone,
E così senza l'uno l'altro esser non osa
Come alma razional senza ragione.

The *kindness* of the heart, understood in the occult anagogical sense, must be understood by the Latin: *gentile* or tending towards the *genti*, altruistic as we would now write; now there's no kindness, or altruism leaving aside from sacrifice of part or all of our *self*, to the happiness of others. The two extremes, *love and altruism* find their opposite in hatred and selfishness. Love and altruism define the limits of the divine powers of the *magician*; hatred and selfishness characterize all that is *sorcery*.

In love, all good is transfused, as all evil in egoism; therefore, the love which implies any sacrifice for others, is divine, and that which is driven by the low ideals of possession is *satannic*: the first one is protected by angels, the second one by demons.

We leave the freedom of ideal love for all mankind to ascetics, religious, and reformers of morals. The mediocre men, those who do not strive to understand an altruism that reaches its manifestation in the complete annihilation of the person who loves, will not understand either the figure of the great revelators, nor those who sacrificed themselves for the triumph of a high idea of justice, nor those who sacrificed their lives in holocaust to public health. The mediocre men must have only known a great and true love, that not rare, neither in the humble hut nor in the palace: the maternal love.

What divinizes the *female* is motherhood: therefore the sterile woman among the ancients was scorned, so the Catholic iconography depicts the Virgin divinized by the presence in her arms of a child and it sanctifies tears in Our Lady of Sorrows.

When two creatures want each other, and they are united by the mayor or the priest, the picture is human. As soon as the wail of a creature seals the union, the deification of the woman begins, her love can only be divine and it can only mark the redemption of any impure love, of any prostitution even blessed by the priest and controlled in the registers of the civil state. The mother's love is neither a calculation, nor a desire: it is a continuous and endless sacrifice of the mind and of the maternal will for the offspring. Her prayer is an evocation of Anael, the greatest love that unites God to his creatures.

Those who have practiced medicine have seen that the intense love of the mother for her creature, in accord with the unshakable faith in an Intelligence-God, has accomplished more miracles than all the miraculous sanctuaries of the world. Maternal love during the period of breastfeeding and until puberty, leads to a continuous transfusion of life, from mother to child, until the two existences are confused in complete dedication to one another.

When the son goes to bridegroom, the mother cries, a woman, any woman, cannot love a man as her mother loves him; if so, the love of the woman for the beloved man would be so angelic and sublime that any dirty sense of flesh would be an offense to purity, and the bride or lover would be confused with the mother and the wedding in the most horrible incest.

The occult philosophy gives love two places: in the brain and in the heart. In the brain, imaginative or calculating, enthusiastic or drunk, love is impure, it is passionate, it is demonic. In the heart, serene, obedient, patient; it is a feeling of abdication and angelic dedication. In physiology we know the relationships that bind the brain to the organs of sexual impurity. Impure love sprouts in them like a desire for vanity: it is Lilith and the Samael destroyers, those who advise and ask to vain people to seize a flower, for leer of power, to trample it like a filth: and every act of this love is a cowardice, in which the heart does not increase its heartbeat that at the moment when bestial pride is satisfied.

But the love of the heart, in which the brain has not put the dull fog of sensuality, is a divine act from which every good is expected.

It is born as an effusion of souls between two natures spiritually completing themselves. It announces itself as a vague feeling of well-being: it grows and increases in intensity as a tacit consent, between two creatures, in a common faith. The first is a *passion*, the second is an *ideal*.

After these few considerations, we pass to the examination of the two principles in practice of natural and divine magic, and in the aberrations of witchcraft.

I.

Those who admit the continuous reincarnations of the human spirit in so many earthly existences, they easily explain the reflection of hatred and love as an organic memory of previous lives.

In the present life it happens to you to see, materially for the first time, a person whose eye, or whose voice, awakens a great feeling of hatred or sympathy. It seems to read in the soul of that man or of that woman as in an open book. He or she has neither said nor done anything to you, yet all of an intimate sense reveals to you that he or she hates you or loves you: who is able to hate you inexorably or to love you tenderly, while a thousand people every day meet you on the way, they travel with you in the same train carriage, they go to the same hotel where you sleep, they eat at the same table where you eat and nobody, just nobody, touches you and it concerns you as much as he or she whom you saw and you see. Is it an instinctive memory of another existence? Mr. Gabriel Delanne, deservedly esteemed for his studies on scientific spiritualism, at the last London congress (June 1898), read an important essay on subsequent lives and the progressive evolution of souls.

The black point of belief in reincarnation is in no memory that in the present life and the generality of men preserves about what has been in the other life.

Delanne answers scientifically: *because the indispensable conditions for renewed remembrance are not fulfilled.* That is to say that certain special conditions for which memory of evnts that have occurred persists even in present life, is not eternal even in life itself. I invite those who deal with natural philosophy to reflect on the influence of physical sensations on memory in *living* man: we can see in the simplest facts that every *physical* sensation cancels the previous ones, and that belongs only to the *psychical* apparatus (cerebral-soul system) the power to evoke them and revive them to memory.

The modern materialistic physiologists make the memory reside in the brain because they have observed that any organic disorder that touches the cerebral lobes produces memory loss up, to aphasia, which is the lack of the memory of words expressing things and common ideas: however, if this is exact in sensist experimentalism, it is not true according to the animist theory and the occult sciences; the material *perception* of the senses is interrupted; the *explication of memory in the physical act* has ceased, but not the potentiality of the soul to retain first impressions[6].

But in order not to enter into boring and abstruse discussions for the unprepared ones, just observe in daily life that every new physical sensation cancels the memory of the previous one: in foods, smells, touches, sounds, in each of the senses dominates the law that the most recent makes us forget the most ancient sensual memory. The bitter is cancelled with the sweet, and, the poet say, ten storms are

---

[6] There is no more interesting question than this. Is the human *soul* with injuries of the cerebral lobes, of the meninges, or with the deep organic lesions, injured? Is it killed? - Materialist philosophy says yes, because man for materialists is the animal organism in its human functions: while, indeed, it is not so. The man struck by paralysis does not speak or does not move. Is the spirit of his inner structure altered by his psyche? Is his spirit destroyed? No - what is destroyed is the bond, that is, the authority of taking the spirit on the body - a plastic bond that can gradually weaken as in volitional and progressing ataxias, or break once and for all as in the instantaneous deaths. Partial paralysis are partial detachments of the authority of possession of the spirit, on the means to manifest its sensations. The effect that the sight of a sick man produces on the healthy people is that the *spirit* of the sick person is *distraught*; while in reality it is only disturbed the means of communication between the spirit and us, and we see its manifestations through the state of its sensory whirlwind.

forgotten with a single ray of sun[7]. Woe to the man, if he did not have the sweet happiness to forget: perennially one would see before the eyes all the strange and repulsive images of his impressions of every kind: enormous torment, which would not hold any comparison to torture! You dream of a delight, just a beat knocked at your door and your eyes open: the images are gone, two hours later no more memory than had enlivened your imagination.

A helping hand helps you in a moment of danger: you are grateful to him, but after the hour of distress, the memory of the act fades away, and your gratitude is annihilated to the point of disappearing entirely. Delanne writes:

"there is no magnetizer who does not know that oblivion on awakening is one of the most constant characteristics of somnambulism. If we put the subject in the somnambulistic state once again, he recovers the memory of what he did and said during sleep. In these conditions it is easy to understand that if the hypothesis of subsequent lives is correct, the recall of the memory of an earlier incarnation is generally impossible. This immense reserve of psychic materials constitutes the substratum of material and moral individuality ... "

What we call the *nature* (Delanne says *character*) of a man or a woman manifested to the thinking life, it would be only the result of the many sensations previously perceived and stored in our psyche or spirit. But the author adds that as

---

[7] What we forget in appearance, our spirit does not forget. The forgotten image apparently assails you at the moment of your involuntary evocation. It has been repeatedly observed that the dying have lucid moments in which everything is clear: this is perfectly true before passing the river Lete, the course of the black waters of oblivion. *Letizia*, seems to come from *lete*, to forget: the man who does not forget is never cheerful.

there are some subjects who in their waking state remember what happened to them in the somnambulistic state, so there existed and there are people who keep the memory of certain facts of the previous life that are very persistent in them. Lamartine remembers that, without ever having visited Judea, he recognized one by one all the most remarkable sites without deceiving himself[8] - Giuliano the Apostate who remembered to have been Alexander the Macedonian - the Damiani (recently died in Naples) that could see himself in his previous existences; a French naval officer who remembered being stabbed in hunting by the Huguenots on the night of St. Bartholomew; a boy from Vera Cruz who distributed medicines remembering perfectly that he had been a doctor - the case of a little girl who died and reborn in the same family and some others.

The occult science - the classical theory of magic - admits in the lower part of the astral current all the souls in formation and imperfect, in constant expectation of reincarnation - but there are also missionary, incarnated spirits outside the evolution of the earthly zone.

They come here just to realize, ignored or known, a mission for the others. Then they go away after having completed comedy. Can these men of higher order have the memory of the past, of the anti-uterine life?

Surely de St. Germain gave proof of this, by telling events of many centuries before; Cardano, classified by Lombroso among the madmen, prided himself on knowing it. And there is no doubt that men who are not famous on earth like the first two previously mentioned, do not know *where they go and where they come from.*

And this is the resolute problem that the Büchner has not been able to solve with the observation sciences only.

---

[8] Those who explain everything with *telepathy* would say that the Lamartine was able to visit and get to know those places in a state of natural lucid somnambulism, sleeping or dozing. This would be a hypothesis, of which it could not be *proved* that it is so.

But returning to our assumption, if we admit the reincarnation, it is possible to explain *fatal loves*. It is possible to preserve the instinctive memory of the effusions of the heart (which are effusions of the spirit in the sweet well-being of a spirit completing itself), in several successive lives, or after several successive lives.

Fatality[9] (or rather the conditions of divine will) will place the two who retain the memory of what they were, clouded by the vague remembrance of an earlier life, in two social conditions on earth that makes their love as a sinful thing: nevertheless the fatal love of the poets has an uncontested explanation in the fact that the two *have to love each other*.

If the only, blind human reason reflects on this, the end of love, according to the divine laws, does not agree with the laws and customs of human society and the epilogue is always tragic. The mere thought that this may be true is terrifying.

You can meet here, embodied, the spirit that in other existences was a very dear and unforgettable companion.

Both of you, if the heavy burden of flab that envelops you, has not completely precluded the memory, can fatally love each other: perhaps they can love each other a second time and this before men is a misfortune that can be translated into adultery, into a violation, into a misfortune, in short, without determination of time or end. Marriages represent in

---

[9] *Fate* is divine, because it represents the result of what was previously prepared. In nature everything is cause and effect: sow and collect. It would be strange if you sowed peas and strawberries came out! The *fatal* of the plant is to give its fruit. The fig tree that does not bear fruit is cursed, because it is cause without effect.

the ordinary of cases the true prostitution of love. Yet these are blessed by the law of men. However, ordinarily all the people of the world living their lives, know that the female free lover who lasts in a long life as a partner with a free man, often it is a testimony of a persistent affection that is sanctified by the heart, if not by the laws. But do not misunderstand: the possible case is not the rule; these loves of pre-existing remembrances are very rare. Morality, the high regulator of civilizations, which Yves Guyot has analyzed with a sense of pessimism, asks who is in such conditions, in the midst of a society that forbids or confuses love with passion, the supreme sacrifice of do not sin, by violating human laws. Societies not founded on respect for the laws, are destructible and decadent. Love for human society is proved only with a sacrifice; by imposing on one's own heart not to violate its customs by violating the conscience of the simples.

The balance of justice is in the hands of Michaël: human justice must portray the divine justice, woe to the truly enlightened spirit that gives rise to the scandal of the violation of the laws: the reformers of public morality come up from there, like angels and light messengers to straighten the cups of balances, when the bestial passions have twisted those cups, never to shake them. The demons, alone, darkened and benighted, can perform works of anarchy. Therefore, the priest, who does not know the spirit of things, says from the altar: *oportet ut scandala non Eveniant...* and refers everything to the Church while the theatre of life is larger and the Church of Christ is the theatre of the world.

We must not believe that true love, the one coming from the heart, is the most difficult in rejecting the possession of the flesh. The most terrible and irresistible devil is the love of the brain.

If everyone could love with heart, the realization of Christianity would be a fact: the kingdom of Christ evoked in the *pater noster* would be realized; the socialist utopia would greet the dawn of the XX century and the earth would be populated with angels. But ... too soon! Here you still love with your brain, in the same way you make peace with cannons, and the reason of every disaster, every pain, every sorrow is the impure love of selfishness.

II.

To the perversion of the Ideal of Love we impute all the terrible satanic legends, the ancient and medieval ones. Leaving aside the ancient stories, on which many uninitiated historians wanted to add their opinions and their inaccurate comments, magnifying all the acts of the sacred lust of the ancient temples, we cannot forget the Roman decadence, in which the imperial society had converted the sunset of the Gods, in a dark and repulsive orgy of pleasures. All the demons of paganism were, from the times of Numa, portrayed in the Fauns and Satyrs: the goat has lent its mask to those bearded apes, symbols of sensual enjoyment.

And a daily visit to the excavations of Pompeii, where you can freely throw an anathema on decadent corruption, should and could be the subject of a book on obscene love in the misfortunes of Roman civilization.

Roman civilization has left the trail of demonic love as the closing seal of imperial corruption in all the expanse of the dazzling and picturesque southern coast of Italy, from Baia to Pesto. Tiberius was called *Caprine*.

It is not known if more for the obscene delights of Capri or for the shamelessness of horned man, who reigned on his own palace: but the people from Pompeii have left, in the scandalous effigy and in the ornaments of the patrician houses, left us the real document of the passion as a rule in the society, evoking from the demons of their religion, all the bestial shamelessness of guilt! Who understands it, can observe that the tradition of the chaldean magic was practiced even in the homes of patricians, slaves and freedmen. Who understand it can observe everything, by visiting the excavations, writings and incisions to plaster, walls, places dedicated to pleasures of the people of the time, and that the vulgar archaeologists do not intend.

The verdant Vesuvius full of woods, covered the whole evocation of the oriental debauchery with a rain of ash, while the Christianity conquered with the blood of the martyrs the right to the angelic love, on the terrible agony of the last three centuries of the empire of the West!

The fall of paganism in the West was a real struggle between the angelic love of Christians and the pagan satyriasis. When the noble center ruling the world of that time was converted into a ugly suburra: when the food and the woman were the only preoccupations of the ruling classes of the pagan society, and the lustful rites and female sacrifices had crossed the temple doors to be inverted in the debility of the aristocratic tables, in the nights of Rome, all society of freedmen, of Praetorians and philosophers prostituted themselves to the delight of cerebral love and of the stomach.

At the same time, white dressed people converted to the God of pure love by the apostolate of Paul of Tarsus, chanted in a virginal aura of divine candour, like a chorus of angels, into the catacombs! While the nights of Rome echoed by the evocations of the demons of impurity, the Christian neophytes prayed to the angels of the new God for the end of the kingdom of the flesh! Paganism had converted the spirit to matter and Christ claimed it.

The adherents of the religion of the angels replaced to the sacrificing orgy of the mysteries of Bacchus, the bloodless sacrifice of the Mass. It is a great act of symbolic magic, to whom the angel of love is not a stranger. I cannot (because the reader, unprepared for the occult truths could misunderstand me) saying more than a few words about what there is of *love* (angelic and demonic) in the celebration of

Mass: the sacrifice that all the books of Catholic prayers say accomplished *without shedding blood*, replaced a part of the ancient mysteries in which the sacrifice was performed with a *bloody* oblation of the victim offering to the Gods.

If the spiritists could evoke from the shadows of Averno, by means of the rotating tables and writing mediums, the spirits of Virgil, Aulus Decius, Horace and Ovid, if they could really make them sing in the eighth rhyme, they would guess something, about this ancient sacrifice and then of the more modern than the Catholics: I only say, *for those who can understand me*, that the celebration of Mass is accomplished with a chalice and a paten, that is, a disk and a glass with the two colors of playing cards, *coins* and *cup*.

You have to ponder that the priest pours the wine that is the blood of the earth in the cup. It consecrates him as *sanctus* between the ascetic faith of the faithful people.

The cleric rings the bell and plays the organ: host and cup rose up, like a dedication and a toast ... then the sacrificer (the priest) *eats and drinks everything*. He does not leave a vestige of the sacrifice, and turning to the people he exclaims: Ite, missa est. *Missa?*

Is it sent? What is IT sent? And where?

But if it is the simple memory of the Last Supper, or the symbolic repetition of the passion, why do the jaws of the sacrificer gobble up the symbolic sacrifice? Those who do not know are not allowed to resolve the riddle of this magical act. This act, performed by an initiated priest, has a terrible value, especially when a whole temple of believing people pray with the priest who is on the altar. The Catholic mystics call it the *sacrifice of the mass*. But, since there is no sacrifice without love, Anaël, the angel of the ideals, is transfused in religious and mystic union in the magical evocation of other times.

But is rare to find a priest initiated into magical philosophy, to its science and practice. While in a religion of *magical* origin such as the Catholic, it should be as a rule. Instead in the whole world it is easy to meet ignorant priests, who dress the priestly dress without any ideal and which are involved into witchcraft with religious practices[10].

The Middle Ages, was so rich in ghosts and bonfires, in dreams, madness and bloody repressions. The Middle Ages saw priests and terrible monks, who for demoniac love, for the concupiscence of the flesh, gave their souls and tonsures to Astaroth, the theologian devil from the caprine foot, the good lord, the good friend of all the sorcerers who frequented the Sabbath or the coven, the infernal dream of the Middle Ages!

On the night before the Sabbath, between midnight and the sing of the rooster proclaiming the dawn, it was known that all the sorcerers and witches would fly, on the heels of brooms, to a festival and to a meeting site headed by this mighty Mr. Astaroth, very resembling in his painting at the Baphomet of the Templar initiates.

---

[10] I do not speak about the priests exercising the profession of the priest: I have known some of them who not only do not know what they are doing celebrating mass, but who do not believe in it, as if the act has no value. Instead they do not realize, in spite of themselves, to be blind instruments of a magical practice that attracts them and submit them. The Mass of the dead people, performed according to the Catholic ritual, when it is recited or sung with all the magical intentionality of the rite, is a real operation of ceremonial psychurgy, from which - to move on to the evocation – the step is very little. If the celebrating priest is very pure, more effective is the spiritual power of the celebrated mass: so the initiate does not have to listen to the Mass recited by an impure priest. But attending the Mass sacrifice he must follow him step by step, interpreting him according to its real meaning, and to the *Orate fratres* he can, if active, to reverse the whole soul of the audience for the purpose of its intentionality, making the operation of the fluidic chain for the benefit of the agent hand. Because it must clearly be distinguished that magic respects all classical religions and catholicism is classic for the pagan and Christian ritual transfused from the first centuries and perpetuated to this day; the magician intelligently uses it.

In the past centuries everyone believed in these strange gatherings of men and devils and from the North to the South of Europe, every region remembered a famous place for the meetings of the witches[11]. Witches and sorcerers flew, singing the *Emen etan, Emen etan*, carried in the air like feathers.

What was done in these nocturnal meetings, I left the free exercise of inventing horrible creatures to the wildest imagination: there the demonic people attended the black mass[12] and while the bells were shaking at the violent jerks of demons, everything, the most libertine, lustful, and obscene that is imaginable but not writable, took place - and the night passed in a horrendous uproar in which the love of the senses, helped by diabolical evocations, inverted every law of morality and religion and faith.

I ask the reader that he is not a poet, to study carefully the phenomenon of this unhappy dream of the Middle Ages, in which the sensual instinct of the common people rebelled against the ascetic oppression of the church and the Christian courts, and while the ones dreamed of nocturnal embraces of the Lord from the caprine foot, the others saw witches and wicked in every person.

---

[11] The Strozzi, cited in the Infernal Dictionary, mentions a chestnut near Piacenza at the foot of which in the radius of a wide circle did not grow grass, because the wizards danced in their orgies. In the south of Italy I heard of a traditional Noce di Benevento on which topic a lot of books were printed, and in Naples a spell recited by certain sorceresses in front of me, ended up with the refrain as a sign of post:...above the water, Under the wind, Under the walnut of Benevento ...

[12] The *Black Mass* was the witchcraft mass with a fantastic and obscene ritual that here is not the case to remember. All the frantic and diabolical legends of the Middle Ages have always brought the Tempter into the churches to disturb the celebration of the mass. Some modern identifies the demon of destruction in *Oros*, whose strong desire is to oppose the Christian God. But demonology is badly understood!

The psychic phenomenon of the Middle Ages deserves careful study: the struggle between the fear of hell and the friends of the Devil, was a satanic struggle. In this one, it is not possible to establish if the judges and friars who condemned people to be burned on the stake, and tortured people who confessed everything under the atrocity of torment, even what they had never thought, they were more insane than the poor idiots and sicks with nerves, who boiled pots and slaughtered children, to steal their throbbing heart! This psychic phenomenon began in the Thebaid with solitaries and hermits. It was perpetuated in the Christian legend and even the monks in the convents had their servant devils[13].

The occult world of human passions, of unbridled and repressed lust, melted and exteriorized itself in the explosion of attempts to corrupting magic in which every sorcerer had a devil by his side and carnal trade with devils and fairies.

The devil was seen everywhere and sensual love evoked him in the legend of St. Anthony Abbate, on which Morelli painted a masterpiece. He saw the devil in every obsession or nervous disorder or alienation of mental faculties.

Mad monks as inquisitors and sorcerers; hell manifested itself for the first time in the *judgments of God*, and then in the fires. Neither the priests nor the friars were saved from the purifying and destroying fire, nor the father repented of denouncing his daughter, nor the husband of having accused the bride, and the lists of the great executions are endless.

And the devil was seen everywhere, because the devil that is the loss of reason in science and in verity, had taken in his spires all the social orders and all classes of citizens. The

---

[13] The Dominicans of Schwerin in Mecklenburg ¬ had a servant devil called Puck. Under the figure of a monkey he turned the spit, swept the kitchen and drew water from the well. A monk wrote: *Veridica relatio de doemonio Puck*! What a good hell!

pact that Dr. Faust in classical legend makes with Mephistopheles is for science, but also for the well-being of sensual life. Remember Margherita.

But the other pacts, those that were said to have been between sorcerers or wizards and Mr. *Astaroth* the terrible demon of possession, aimed at material happiness of the senses: this has passed beyond the limits of the Middle Ages and it has arrived to us to impose itself in the popular traditions of all countries. Famous in France was the hysterical epidemic of the sisters of Ludun, in which a whole monastery was spirited. A priest of a very good nature called Urbano Grandier was accused of having *bewitched* the nuns, infiltrating a true epidemic of lasciviousness and libertinism in the convent. Urban Grandier was burned alive and his last words were the following ones: *I am innocent*!

But tortured people were much more innocent of torturers and executioners: the human mind under the empire of ignorance evoked the diabolical adventures of debauchery and violence!

But was this psychic and demonic epidemic of the Middle Ages true? Did not then exist any practice that could *externalize*, as we say today, the *fluidic body* of witches and sorcerers to go to enjoy the devils, or to be enjoyed by the embrace of the goat, idealizing all the low sensual cravings of the pacts with the devil?

The phenomenon can have many scientific explanations - it is undeniable, however, the use of ointments or pomades that generated powerful exaltations of the fluidic body in the pathological sleep of a night consecrated by tradition to the celebration of nefarious rituals.

Today so much was written about hashish and opium but the exact formulas of the ointments used by sorcerers and wizards, are very rare, nor it is advisable to put them into use. The inebriating substances all act on the sensory centers and therefore on the perisprit or astral body. Making use of it, it is a way of facilitating the experimentation of one's own exteriorization, but it is not a scientific and progressive means of improvement. The excitement of the centers with substances such as the Spanish fly and the hemlock is a permanent danger to the life of reason in the human body; and the lustful delirium is more terrible than any delirium caused by use and abuse of alcohol.

The Indian cannabis put in some combinations of plant narcotic extracts (the black poppy, for example) and it is a very powerful agent for somnambulic self-hypnosis, but hashish is known to practitioners. With the flower of local cannabis (the pollen collected in the moon of June) and a mixture of wine alcohol and hops flowers is possible to produce one of these powerful and less harmful energizers, of which I will give the recipe on another occasion.

These ointments and these narcotics of the empirical and learned alchemy their own evoked concupiscent demon in the shameless dreams of carnal love. I do not recommend to any person to evoke the demon Astaroth. The one who wants to evoke him, will evoke in the mental disorder the whole Middle Ages of lies and guilt.

III.

Giovanni Boccaccio writes in his own Commentary on the Divine Comedy: *The Leopard*[14] *is very light in her body. She is wonderfully vague with the blood of the goat.* What prevented Alighieri's spiritual ascension was the burning lust, incarnated by the Leopard. Boccaccio describes her as wonderfully vague, with the goat's blood;

perciocchè siccome il becco è lussuriosissimo animale, così per l'usare questo vizio più lussurioso si diviene[15].

All the love of the brain has its altar in witchcraft which is the magic of evil. The pig from which the graceful Adonis was killed was this and the Leopard is the most terrible enemy of the divinization of men.

I talk to you as an illuminated man, and perhaps the people of contemporary society will smile at the polite threat of abstinence from the pleasures of the senses. But magic teaches it and remembers it, that every impure act determines the fall of an angel from Heaven.

---

[14] The exact term used in Dante Alighieri is *Lonza* (the Editor).

[15] In the *Mondo Secreto* (2nd year, issue I) was published the effigy of the templar Baphomet. The monster with its hooked horns, with its phallic protuberances and its goat's leg is man and goat. This figure was said to be adored by the Templars. But all the gentle times had their part of sacred lust. The priapic festivals, the mysteries of Eleusis, the saturnals, were rituals. All the forms of the devil in all religions had a goat. The Moloch of the Ammonites had the head of a cow; Belfegor of the Jews was very closer to the goat. So it is sure that the goat was always kept as an expression of lasciviousness, especially in the symbolism of ancient religions. The way in which the goat is involved in the ritual of magical realization, it is reserved for those who study magic. And this, just not to generate errors

What I now mention, is one of the highest mysteries of initiation into absolute truth. The dream of every profane is the possession of the female: laws, religions, public morality extinguish that fire incubating in every brain. But if in magic someone proceeds with the sacred tingling of the flesh, it's possible to slide into the criminal drop of the greatest of faults: the black magic.

As there are two loves, two spells coexist, that of the virtue and that of the sin; the holy and the diabolic, the white and the black, the magic of the heart and that of the head, the first radiant light, and the second one horned like the goat mentioned by Boccaccio a few words earlier. Of the two loves the first is eternal; it lasts through many earthly existences, and if in some of them it remains sleepy, in others it flares up. But the second one is for a short time,

> *...assai di lieve si comprende,*
> *Quando in femmina fuoco d'amor dura*
> *Se l'occhio e il tatto spesso non raccende*[16].

If pagan mythology could be literally read, Jason loved three women Isifile, Medea and Creusa with his brain. but Ero loved Leandro with her heart. The angel of pure love is Anael, the two demons, male and female, of sensuality are Samael, the angel of death and Lilith, the beautiful and seductive Goddess of succubus[17].

---

[16] Cited from Dante Alighieri's Comedy, Purgatory, VIII, 78 (the Editor).

[17] *Incubus and succubus*: what are they? Doctors say that they are the symbols of violent indigestion, whose effects are obtained in the spasm of sleep of those who have not digested. But these doctors confuse the bump of Adam with the flute of Silene. Doctors want to have ideas of *incubus and succubus* in hospitals, where Incubus and succubus do not go. Demonologists say that they are spirits of male or female demons who make love with the sons or

Anael is the creator; Samael is a destroyer: the ancient Jewish traditions tell that the serpent of the adamitic seduction, which had the head of a man, is Samael. In fact, the impure act of animal love tends to produce, through the embrace, new masses for the sickle of death: if the spirits did not become flesh, the sickle would certainly not reach them.

But horrible to visit is all the hell of ignoble human passions! Dante fears the Leopard, and the great obstacle to magical asceticism is in that vague smell of goat, taking all the miserable bodies of human society. For this smell, social customs teach us two morals, the first one that preaches respectful observance of the woman of others publicly, and the other one that leaves in the heart of every man burning, the little proudly fire that advises to hunt down the attractive woman, like the hunters of the birds in the woods.

And every woman, who in the example of the libertinage of the honest gentlemen feels for a long time to graze her imagination, even with the appearances of Lucrezia in public, she would in private complain of the villain who did not violente her pleasantly ; and the hispid man who did not show her the slobbering sneer of the goat, in the darting of his two cupid eyes, he would be even worse than the worst of the friars - who have, from a long time, good names for seekers of flesh to send to Muhammad's paradise.

Therefore the contrast of the two morals: the first tries to prevent what the second desires and provokes in secret. And the snots to all the small industries of the evil and the art of divination are lighted, from cartomancy to the bad art of *filters*, in order to possess not the heart, but the brain of a man or woman whom one desires with the brain.

The legendary struggle between the faithful angels and the rebels, is the struggle between the two morals.

---

daughters of men. But there are no doubts about the existence of some *spirits* with a strong tendency of lasciviousness, although there are examples of sorcerers and witches who at night visited (and they *visite*) their darlings, under fluidic forms. What incredible stories!

Anael, the angel of purity is against Astarte, the Goddess of shamelessness and sensuality. Miszraël, *the help of God*, comes down to prevent falls: a hand that trembles because it approaches the violation of the law of the spirit, finds in this ray of Divinity the angelic hand that leads it in the refuge of mystical faith and absolute goodness. So the eagerly people return to God: the angel Miszraël gives them the courage of repentance and tells in the ear of disillusioned or deceived women the sweet word of forgiveness and makes her promise not to sin ever again, *ever*, because who is with the spirit not returns to the chasm of passion and sin.

The drama of the consciences is the most terrible: the men and the women who have felt teared and disenchanted their afflicted soul by a betrayal, or who have never cried like in the moment that they have returned to the calm of the spirit after an orgy of thoughts and sinful invocations, or who plagued faith in humanity on the day when they coldly saw its cowardice, they have their terrible moment; their drama of the soul, in which, as Jacob fighting with the Spirit, they ask the angel of the rescue of God, faith, peace, forgiveness. And Miszraël does not wait. The epilogue of the drama of the spirit brings the stigmata of pain, and the pain ages and the aged spirits do not sin!

Some stormy lives, pierced ten times by passions, alternating delights and pains, come to the most sentimental asceticism and find their natural refuge in faith: when Severino Boethius was in prison, the consolation of philosophy came to him like a balm: it was Miszraël who opened his wings on the catastrophe of that life, born in the pomp and set in the prison.

What do you grieve, or wounded soul from misfortune? Of the lost wealth? Of the joy disappeared in your house? Of the betrayal of the creature you wanted only for you? Everything is vanity, everything is dream, everything is insane fantasy: the truth is in the life of the spirit, above all the mud of impure matter.

Pray, scourge yourself, refrain...close your soul in the mystic veil of faith and hope. "The weakened soul feels the friendly voice in the angel: who cares more than the matter that betrayed her? But the mocking demon, the lord of Matter, horned or lascivious like the billygoat, *Mr.* Astaroth echoes and sneers:- Good guy! Poor beast, you become a friar for not having become a lucky devil ... let yourself be enchanted by the beautiful words, my empire is this.

Here is the matter, I'm the one who commands: remember Trimalcione's trumpet warning of lost hours! Your life is too short, and a minute passing without enjoyment and it will not reappear. If you wanted to sing with angels why did you come into my muddy empire? In theatres, from the Melodrama to the popular tragedy, from the *Trovatore* to the sensational dramas of the Arenas, the spectators have taken the form of witches and sorceress. A cave, on a solitary site near a cemetery, some smoky and gloomy walls. A pot boils on a crackling wood fire; in the pot dead bones, bat's blood, the heart of some killed child, and all with verbena and sage and poisonous mushrooms.

In a corner of the cave, bones and skulls of feline animals, a cat nailed alive to the wall, and who still struggles and moans in long terrible agony.

The head of an owl stuck to the rock, some poisonous snakes in a red black vase of terracotta. Glip hair. The black robe, on which the red signs of violence and hatred. The witch holds her wand and calls the terrible demon of lust and death. Samael is there.

Spectators do not quiver. Someone laughs. At the end of this century of enlightenment, a civil public would be foolish to believe all this show of fantastic evocation. Yet science, progressing, will demonstrate two things:

1) That the witchcraft curse is perfectly a possibility, of the human psyche inverted to evil;

2. That the evil and sorcery, in the times of progress, can be accomplished without the hearts of newborns, nor

dust of the dead, without caverns in the rocks and without the flash of lightning at midnight. And that you can be a witch or a sorcerer, living the elegant life of good society, and preserving all the appearance of modest people.

IV.

The "envoûtement", of which so much has been said in the modern books and that the experiences of the externalization of the fluidic body published by the Colonel de Rochas already begin to make possible in the eyes of the profane scholar, is a spell that was made and done for love and for death in two different ways.

In this case, I will tell you all the way to do the spell, to make people understand what it is, but I will not say the secret that the practioners use to make sure that the result is unavoidable.

They take a piece of new wax, that is, not yet worked (if it is a curse of love), or a piece of candle burned near a corpse (if it is a curse of death) and make an image, baptizing it with the name or with the names of the person on whom to act; then, by means of a pin, they pierce the heart or the genitals of the man or woman they want to subjugate. And they repeat the operation so many times until the effects are visible. This evil of love or "involtamento" can have two purposes:

1)To shake the person under a spell, just to make him go to the person who desideres him;

2. To Make the person under a spell impotent at sexual love. This second fact corresponds to a manner of evil in the witch scope. It is known as make a knots or to knot. It is clear that if the operation were accomplished as I wrote, everyone would be able, in such a simple and economic way, to kill a man and to make a woman fallen in love ; but the secret is in that baptism of the wax doll that few people know well.

Some went to bad priests who, for little money, have not been ashamed to desecrate their holy ministry. And they have repeated the baptism of the person on whom the curse was addressed to the statue, to make the sorcerer sure to act effectively. Others have kneaded the victim's hair with wax; Others with something worse. But all these methods are empirical. There is a way, (and the reader will easily understand why it does not have to be manifested by those who guess) that establishes the exact correspondence between the wax figurine and the person on which you want act, so that every act performed on the person's mask is reproduced on the person himself. Paracelsus used this process to obtain his wonderful healings and the method turned to evil, produces evil.

This establishing *a real correspondence between an image and the person that the image represents*, has been studied with great care: the word *envoûtement* must be understood in its importance, because it refers to the face of the haunted man. So *in-voltamento* (the French *envoûtement*) means correspondence by resemblance, because the greater or lesser resemblance of the doll to the person on which one wants to act, makes the effect more or less probable.

In Italian, as I have also said elsewhere, we do not find a word corresponding to the French word exactly; there is *evil and spell*: the one that comes closest to it is *fattura*, in the meaning of witchcraft performed against a person for the features or appearance of him, and it is a word of the excellent Italian language of Sacchetti and Boccaccio: so there is also the verb *to bewitch*.

But *envoûter* for people who love the exotic more than what comes from their own country, must be better digestible instead *fattura*, a word fallen into the mouth even to the common people in that meaning, and it would happen that, for the only fact of the luck of the words, the doctors would not understand it. The procedures to perform the evil are various and in these *fatture* for love we find all the phases of magnetization at the distance. The adepts of black magic use evocations of *demònii* (I say *demons* to indicate the demons with hostile tendencies to man) or strong *spirits* of materiality that come to produce a whirlwind in the fluidic organism of the bewitched.

They help the evocations with ceremonial magic acts, with the most energetic *seals* and *signs* in manifestations of power in the distance, with *powerful words* that black magicians can pronounce as issuers fluidic forces and fluidic wills and with sounds or noises to produce such vortices to impose a weak creature in the invisible canvas of evil.

Just making a wax doll and baptizing it with a baptism of a priest, does not detract and does not do much. First of all, the bad priest must be a black magician, otherwise the simple act of administering a sacrament to a body without a soul, puts him out of the holy liturgy of the church and his baptism and the state of correspondence are void. Putting, kneaded with wax, hair or nails or blood of the alleged victim is not effective if - in the operation - all things are not heated with the active sauces of the *coercive* spirits of the will of others, or *perturbing* spirits of sensuality. These demons, as with prayers the angels come down, for curses they hurl themselves against the person who, unprepared to receive them, does not reject them and he would tend to reject them in vain.

I do not write the novel and what I write serenely, must be understood serenely; today only a few of the profane people take care of it, but if it is established into medical schools that the curse is a truth and that many inexplicable diseases to the best diagnostic doctors are produced from which the official science does not want to hear as certainties, modern codes should take care of black magicians and its excellence Zanardelli would copy the laws of Rotari of the Lombards or the most modern, to put into practice the cremation of the evil men and witches!

These evils of love, often imperfectly made by unable and inexperienced witches, produce other physical disturbances that have nothing to do with the *passion* they want to generate and the people they desire are often beaten to death. I met a young lady who fell sick with an inexplicable illness a few days after expelling a pretender from her house. Her illness began with a lucid dream, which was always present in her eyes in her frightening reality.

She dreamed of resting in her bed, and that a hand had settled on her chest, a hairy hand, like a bear's paw. The hand became heavier and the pressure terrible: in the dream she grasped the hand, to try to get rid of it; she opened her eyes and the face of an old and toothless woman approached her face, snickering some incomprehensible curses... the awakening was painful.

Eight days later the dream was repeated, varying its shape. The spasm was identical; but the old woman, the same old woman, tore at her heart with a bloody knife and said softly: *you will not love that X, and X will be your passion.*

From that day the girl did not have an hour of peace: she did not love and did not want the boyfriend of that time, but her health was reduced to its limits and for five years she crossed the antechambers of the most important doctors. To the one who told it, the story seemed to be a sissy stuff; several have said she was gone crazy; indeed she has been the victim of a badly executed love curse but powerfully accomplished.

The patient's mental faculties gradually worsened, and two nights before she died she once again dreamed of invisible visitor who told her the same words of five years before! Is it a phenomenon of madness or is it an act of violence that wicked people have used against her?

Demons or evil spirits, who routinely hurl themselves against people who designate themselves to maleficent victims, are not frog *spirits* - they are the vitalized creatures of the astral who strike the perispirit or fluidic body of a victim, arriving to kill her! At the time of Catherine de Medici in France under the reign of Henry III, Charles IX and Henry IV, this way to bewitch to death, it was widespread. It seems that in the Middle Ages in Italy the method had to be widely known, because a recent study has put in view a spell that Galeazzo Visconti wanted to make against Pope John XXII, so that Dante Alighieri who seems to have become a very expert magician, was questioned if he wanted to baptize (or better, the Italian incantare), the silver statue of the Pope[18].

But in general historical memories, mention should be made of the process of the *Nun of Monza* in which the Lady, whom Alessandro Manzoni deals with in the *Promessi Sposi*, confessed to the judges that through the grate of the locutory, her lover gave her to kiss an object of indistinct shape. This object put in her veins such a fire that from that day, although she did not want to go to meetings with her lover, she felt pulled by force and against her will[19].

This already belongs to a second way of overcoming the resistance of the weak women touched by witchcraft - and it is part, without being perfectly, of very ancient love *filters* or drinks. The *filters* are real magic poisons, elixirs that act on the brains of people who are not mad and that absorb them. The *filters* are used in two ways: either by making the man or the woman drink it, or by spreading them on the sites where the victim usually remains. From this we deduce that the filters are composed of those poisons impossible to find in chemical analyzes, of which the Borgias were said to be holders, or of psychic poisons that reach the brain through the nostrils. The secret of manipulation of these energetic and powerful filters is in the

---

[18] L. ESQUIEU, *Papa Giovanni XXII e le scienze occulte*; and in the *Rivisita d'Italia* (fascicolo 15 maggio 1898) and essay of Mr. Della Giovanna on *Dante the magician*.

[19] V. TULLIO DANDOLO, *La Monaca di Monza*.

determination of the powerfully magnetized will of the sorcerer on the distillation of organic, animal and vegetable substances, directed at coercing a weaker will. The ancient almanacs and *the books of wonderful secrets* have many recipes for the manufacture of *filters*: but the most powerful filter is the *kiss of satan*, to which the Nun of Monza alludes. This spell was done in the following way.

A large medal was built, generally of copper, like that of the saints, which opened itself into two matching discs. The outer face showed the most stubborn demonic and priapic figures in relief or engraved, and in the inside a true diabolical reliquary, impregnated with smells and filtering waters that act on the brains of the unfortunate woman.

The object *must be kissed*, and it was held as close as possible to the person's mouth and nostrils. The poisoning was done this way.

Those who know about modern hypnotism studies know about the latest experiments done in France and reproduced and controlled in many laboratories. We refer to those made by Luys and his collaborators on the curative action of medicines at a distance. Well, the simplest and initial thing is already within everyone's reach; *with the perispirit or fluidic body or astral body you can drink the toxic or healthy properties of things naturally useful or poisonous to our body.*

Just for now it is not known that this, that to put in contact a poison with the fluidic body of a person, he must be placed in a state of sleepwalking. While a very simple method belongs to the ranks of the *secrets* of operative magic (annoying *secrets* for who do not want to hear nothing about them in times when everyone thinks to know everything and that everything must be told) with which you can approach the fluidic body of any person without putting it into a hypnotic state. The recipe book of these psychic poisons would take large proportions if they were to be written. The powerful poisons of the three kingdoms find their place:

from hemlock to henbane, from stramonium to potassium cyanide, from mushrooms to viper venom; nothing of them has arrested the poisoning passion that has found in witches and evil hired females, maleficent projection instruments over poor and innocent creatures. The *filters* are for love but the name of *filter* is also taken in the larger sense of evil drink and contains all the ingredients, from the actual poison to the hypothetical poison; from the extract of poisonous herbs to the dust of dead bones.

Having drunk a poison prepared like this, its lethal effect is sure; but black sorcerers or wizards, powerful in their practices, do not make their *filters* drink nor strew the food of their enemies. It is enough that the filter water is spread in a place where the victim can insensibly breathe a particle and the effect is obtained.

Is it the poison or the vapour of poisons that kills or enchants or perturbs? Not always. As for spells, so for *filters*. Those demons refused by official science come out from poisonous water - and the victim is struck with no defense! The Rose † Cross of France assumed the mission to fight the evil, everywhere, and new spiritual tribunal, to assist the defense of the innocent: high ideal!

V.

So is all this possible? Is not it the resurrection of a dream? Is truth. The future will prove it as a scientific thing, and the people who now laughs, making fun of us, will no longer laugh. In order to free oneself from every curse of the love of another's brain, one must not desire vice; and one has to love like the angels, with the heart.

Anaêl is the great angel of the love of God. The churches make him their sacrament, by invoking fidelity and purity in conjugal love. Miszraël is the consolation of the afflicted people. Samael is the angel of death; Lilith the demon of Lust. Astaroth, described on a dragon with a viper in his hand, is the demon of materiality, the most popular among black magicians and witches. An epicureian devil, a good devil, but always a devil.

I have not the artist's pen to describe it; but who knows how the medieval psyche turned the demonic evocation of this philistine idol into the spider's web of a bestial mystery, can do it without me.

Astaroth who served as a sinister adornment to all the religious fables and the exorcists of the obscurantism of the reason of faith, which lasted in Europe until the eighteenth century, he was sought everywhere. Now he is evoked from a long time, the great Lord of the Sabbath! Spiritism invokes souls who moralize and forget the obsessions of eighteen demonomani centuries !

After the fall of the gentile gods, human reason has shattered the simulacra of the passions in the seducing demons, the names of which taken from the Jew, the Phoenician, the Syriac and languages never heard, pervaded the conscience of all fearful as ghosts polyform. But those who today are assiduous in disbelief, experimenters and philosophers of the sensuous nature, they must not forget that to the cohort of the mocking demons, *representatives of the fight against the official faith in all the ages*, they owe the intellectual revolution of our times that the angels of the logic of science already greet! But as long as there is matter, a part of humanity loves with demons, reversing the full potential of the psyche to selfishness.

Humanity struggles between Angels and Demons, between sin and vice: between concupiscent desire and love in God, the love of the heart, which is sacrifice in front of the other that is beloved and that the church bans as a sin.

To free oneself from the love of the brain, one must pray to Anaél, in the following manner:

"O angel, you who are the love of God, the human imagination is filthy with the burning sensations of the flesh, make me not love for pleasure and that when my flesh sins my spirit flights to you».

In fact, hygiene teaches that when the man combines the feeling of the with all the refinement of spiritual enjoyment, the act do not follow nature and it has pathological consequences. The spirit invokes the angel, and the flesh the demon; here is the eternal contrast of good and evil, of the ideal and of matter!

Iconographic Appendix

First Edition, Naples 1898

Angeli e Demònii
dell' Amore

del Dott. GIULIANO KREMMERZ

Amori fatali,
Amori colpevoli,
Maleficii d' amore.

NAPOLI
LIBRERIA DETKEN & ROCHOLL
Piazza del Plebiscito
1898

Third Edition, Naples 1921

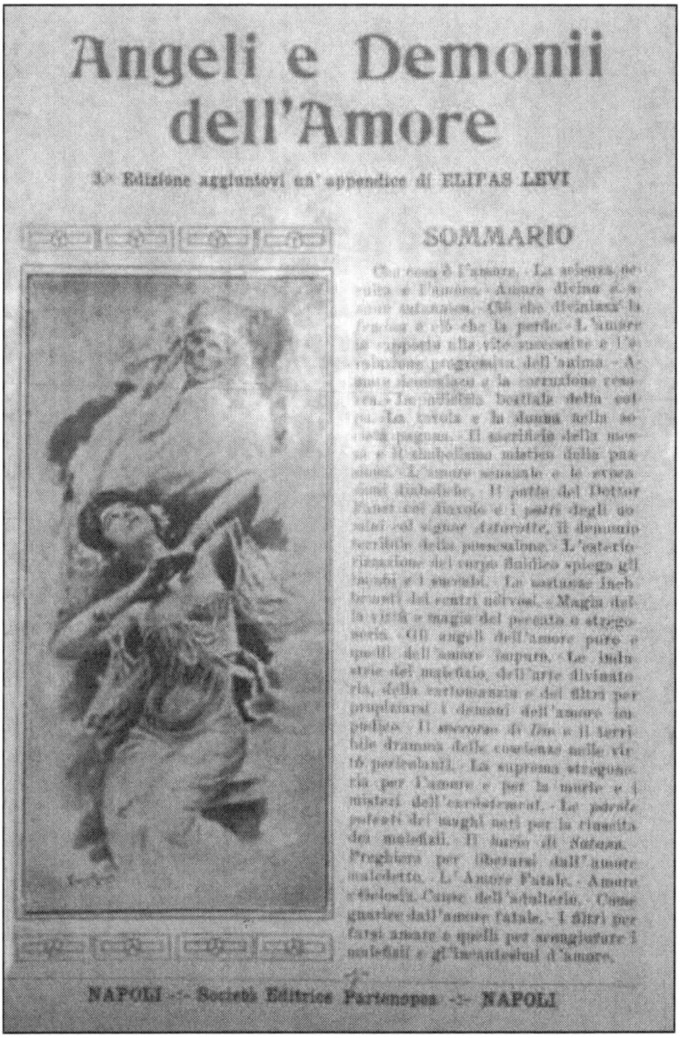

Fourth Edition, Naples 1946

GIULIANO KREMMERZ

ANGELI E DEMONI DELL'AMORE

con un'appendice di ELIFAS LEVI sui Filtri d'Amore

SOMMARIO

Che cosa è l'amore. La scienza occulta e l'amore. Significato allegorico della Beatrice di Dante. La Sapienza degli eletti. Amore divino e amore satanico. Ciò che divinizza la femina e ciò che la perde. L'amore in rapporto alle vite successive e l'evoluzione progressiva dell'anima. Amore demoniaco e corruzione cesarea. Impudicizia bestiale della colpa. Il sacrificio della messa e il simbolismo mistico della passione. L'amore sensuale e le evocazioni diaboliche. Il fenomeno psichico del medioevo. Il patto del dottor Faust col Diavolo e i patti degli uomini col sig. Astarotte. Il demonio terribile della possessione. L'esteriorizzazione del corpo fluidico spiega gli incubi e i succubi. Le sostanze inebrianti dei centri nervosi. Magia della virtù e magia del peccato o stregoneria. Gli angeli dell'amore impuro. L'inferno delle basse passioni [illegible]. Le industrie del maleficio e dell'arte divinatoria della cartomanzia e dei filtri per propiziarsi i demoni dell'amore impudico. Il soccorso di Dio e il terribile dramma delle coscienze nelle virtù pericolanti. La suprema stregoneria per l'amore e per la morte e i misteri dell'envoûtement. Le parole potenti dei maghi neri per la riuscita dei malefizi. Il bacio di Satana. Preghiera per liberarsi dall'amore maledetto.

Fifth Edition, Naples 1947

Dr. GIULIANO KREMMERZ

ANGELI E DEMONI
DELL'AMORE

AMORI FATALI - AMORI COLPEVOLI - MALEFIZII D'AMORE

con una nota introduttiva sulla Vita, l'Opera
e le Attività Magiche del Kremmerz
di A. VERNIERO

NAPOLI - SOCIETÀ EDITRICE PARTENOPEA - NAPOLI

INDEX

Foreword...pp. 5-6

Angels and Demons of Love...........................pp. 7-41

Iconographic Appendix...............................pp. 43-46

Index...pp. 47.

Made in the USA
San Bernardino,
CA